You are a designer

What is the use of change?; 85; good
— Suitable for research work.

Tevet 5772

Schools Council Design and Craft Education Project

This project was set up in 1968 at the University of Keele and continued there for five years with a Schools Council grant of £60,850. Its main aims were to survey the range of craft activities in secondary schools, to identify educational objectives in craft teaching, and to examine methods of validating the effectiveness of craft curricula in attaining those educational objectives.

Project team

Director: Professor S John Eggleston
Senior Research Fellows: A R Pemberton, D Taberner
Field Officer (from 1971): Louis Brough
Writer/Editor (from 1971): Russell J Hall

You are a designer
Schools Council Design and Craft Education Project

Edward Arnold

© Schools Council Publications 1974

First published 1974
by Edward Arnold (Publishers) Ltd
41, Bedford Square, London WC1B 3DQ

Edward Arnold (Australia) Ltd
80 Waverley Road, Caulfield East
Victoria 3145, Australia

Reprinted 1978, 1982, 1985, 1986

ISBN: 0 7131 1804 0

All Rights Reserved. No part of this publication may be reproduced, stored in a retrieval system, or transmitted in any form or by any means, electronic, mechanical, photocopying, recording or otherwise, without the prior permission of Edward Arnold (Publishers) Ltd.

Illustrations in this book are by Roy Schofield

Reproduced and printed by photolithography and bound in Great Britain at The Bath Press, Avon

Contents

Introduction	7
What is Designing?	8
Situation	24
Brief	26
Investigation:	30
Function:	34
size	34
strength	36
adaptability	36
access	37
Ergonomics	38
Materials	40
Construction	42
Appearance	45
Cost	47
Time	48
Solution	49
Realization	53
Testing	56
Design in Daily Life	59

Acknowledgments

The publisher's thanks are due to the following for permission to use photographs in this book:

John Maltby Ltd (p. 43, bottom)
British Aircraft Corporation (p. 45, top)
Gordon McLeish & Associates Ltd (p. 45, bottom)

Introduction

We are all designers. We design things to use, things to eat and things to do. When you are working out how to make a kennel for your dog, or the best way to redecorate your room, you are *designing*. And when you plan how you are going to spend your weekend—the meals you would like to eat, the clothes you will buy—you are *designing*.

There are many things you have to think about when tackling a design problem. Some of these you will find in this book. Not all of them will affect every problem—so you will need to decide what is important in each case.

You will find it useful first of all to read the whole of this book to get to know the design process fully, but it is also a *reference book* to be used when you think it will be helpful. In other words, in most of your designing you won't need to start at the beginning of this book and work right the way through. Instead you will be able, with the help of the list of contents on page 5, to use just those sections which are relevant to your design problem or those about which you wish to be reminded.

Question: How am I going to spend the next decades of my life?

What is designing?

Man is continually making changes in the world around him. He may take something away or add something that wasn't there before. He may join things together or take them apart. Whatever he makes or does has an effect of some sort on him, on his fellow men and on his surroundings. Sometimes these effects are small, sometimes they are very large indeed.

Here are some examples of the sort of changes we can make.

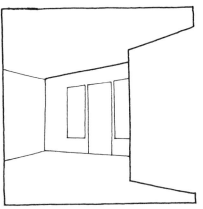 

You may think that some changes that have been made are good while others are not so good. But one thing is certain: before any change was made, someone, somewhere, first of all saw a *reason* or felt a *need* for that particular change and then set about making a *plan of action* to bring it about.

By using this book you will be able to understand how reasons and *needs* can be recognized and how a *plan of action* can be made and put into operation. In other words, you will be able to appreciate not only how things around us change and evolve but also how *you* can contribute (and indeed do already contribute) in all kinds of ways. This, in broad terms, is what we mean by *designing*.

What actually happens when you design? Follow this example and see if you can trace the way in which the problem is solved and the stages that are passed through.

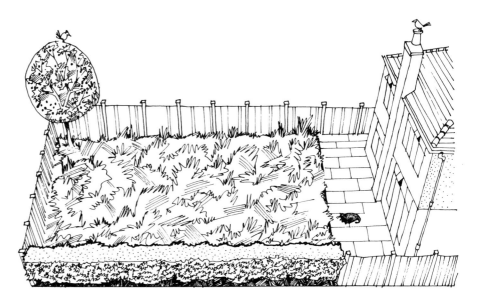

Here is a new house . . . and a garden.

It is rare for a family to move into a new house where the garden has been designed; this is usually left to the new occupants. This one, anyway, is nothing but an empty patch of ground. What can be done about it?

In deciding how to lay out a new garden you would probably start by thinking about what it is going to be used for. It would help if you wrote down a list of the things that might be done there.

The size of the garden will obviously influence its use. But whatever the size you should be able to get pleasure from it—perhaps by playing games there or because of the flowers and trees it contains.

In order to enjoy a garden fully and look after it easily you must be able to walk about it. This is something you have to take into consideration when planning the layout; it would not be a good idea to have to walk through the flower beds! At some stage, therefore, you will have to think about paths and this will lead you to consider a number of questions:

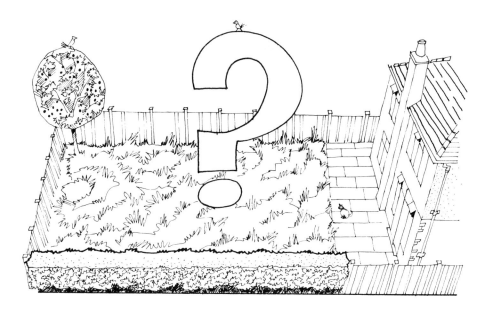

— Who will use the paths most?

— What will the paths be used for?

— Where will the paths be needed?

— Do paths alter the proportions of the garden?

— Do paths need to be straight?

— Do paths need to have parallel edges?

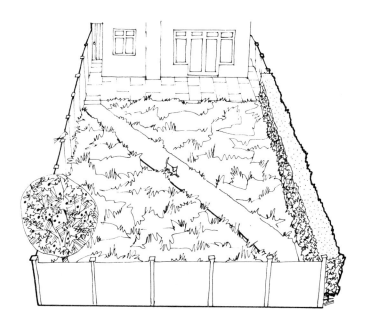

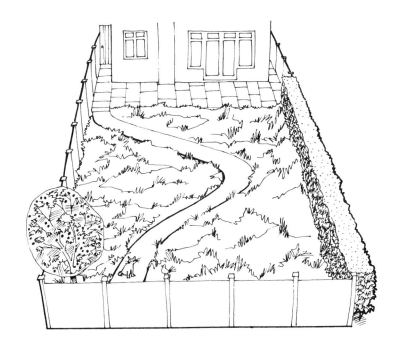

- **What materials are available with which to make the paths?**
- **Is their surface texture important?**
- **What about colour?**
- **How much will the paths cost?**

Let us suppose that, for various reasons, you decide that your exact need is for an *inexpensive path* made of a *hard-wearing, multi-coloured* material that could be *altered in shape and size* if desired.

Does this seem impossible to achieve?

Consider some of the materials that could be used for paths:

Grass Can wear out with heavy use. Becomes muddy in wet weather. Needs regular attention. Only available in green.

Stones Loose, uneven and easily kicked out of place. Could damage mower if kicked onto lawn.

Paving slabs Although rather heavy, could be moved to allow garden layout to be changed.

'Tarmac' Hard-wearing. May need special laying equipment. Permanent.

Concrete Hard-wearing. Quite easy to lay but may need help of friends. Permanent.

You could probably think of other materials. But which of the above ideas seem most suitable?

Often the most suitable answer is a combination of several ideas. In this case concrete offers a hard-wearing surface that could be multi-coloured if necessary (by using coloured stones when mixing).

But you will remember that we wanted a path that could be changed in shape and size—large areas of concrete cannot be moved easily.

The answer seems to be to use fairly small slabs. These can be bought. But how much would they cost? Imagine that the path is required to cover an area of 10 square metres. Suppose ordinary grey, half-metre square slabs cost 40p each. You would need forty slabs and this would cost £16. If you wanted coloured or unusually shaped slabs the cost would be much higher.

Perhaps it would be cheaper to make your own slabs. To cover 10 square metres you would need approximately 1 ton of sand and stones, (let's assume it costs about £3) and 4 cwt of cement, say at 75p a hundredweight. Allowing £2 to cover the cost of materials to make the moulds this would give a total cost of approximately £8.

You could therefore save quite a lot by making your own slabs . . . and by using different mould patterns and coloured cements you have a much wider choice of shape and colour.

While deciding on the shape, size and colour of the slabs you can see that another major design problem has emerged—not only do you have to choose an appropriate slab you must also decide how to make it. You have to design and make a mould.

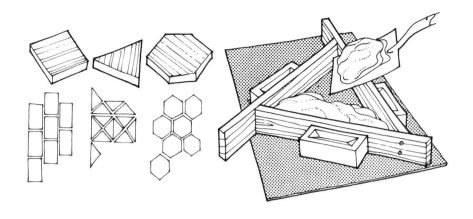

When this is done the concrete can be mixed and poured to make the slabs. The laying of the slabs would need to be planned and carried out fairly carefully to make sure that the paths were level and of the required shape.

Great satisfaction may be had from a job well done. How can you tell if the job is well done? ... By seeing how well the path meets your original requirement.

Now let's look back at what you have done so far.
In arriving at this ...

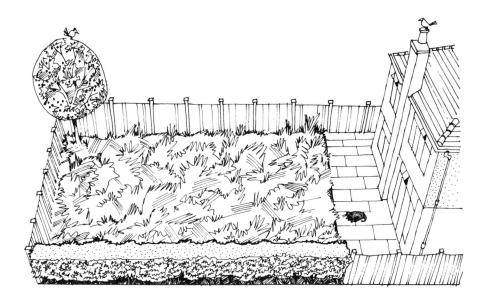

from this . . . what has happened?

situation

You started with an empty garden. You could say that at the beginning you had a *situation*.

brief

When you looked at this situation you discovered a need—the need for a walking area. In a design problem this statement of the original need is usually called a *brief*.

investigation

The brief was examined more closely so that the requirements could be *specified* in more detail. Questions were asked and answered and a range of ideas was considered. Some of these were sketched. At this stage you could say that an *investigation* was taking place.

solution

The time came when a firm decision had to be made and one idea chosen. You could say that a *solution* was selected.

realization

After checking that all the materials were available and sizes and shapes were correct you were able to make the path—to *realize* your solution to the original problem.

testing

After completing the work it was possible to sit back and admire it. It was tried out by other people as well as those actually responsible for the work. In this way you could say that the finished path was *tested*.

You can see from this example that designing may be divided into several stages. When you are designing and making something from the beginning you will find yourself following a more or less similar pattern. This pattern is called a *design process*.

You may not always follow a design process from start to finish. Work in some of the stages may already have been done for you. For example, someone else may have already found a need which you can turn into a design brief. Or they may give you a complete brief. Sometimes your realization stage may involve repairing or buying something instead of making it.

Design often starts with an existing idea or object that needs to be improved or developed. Next year's motor cars, for example, will be developed from those that already exist. Furniture, too, is usually designed in this way.

The way in which you apply a design process depends on what the problem is and what you wish to accomplish; and this may be affected by time, materials or your own interests. You may not always need to include all the stages. Or you may deal with them in a different order. On some occasions certain stages may be completed very quickly, others may take a long time to work out.

You can see that each design problem needs individual consideration before a suitable *plan of action* can be drawn up. A few moments thought before tackling a problem can often save time (and money!) later on as well as leading to better results.

Everything that is made—from mousetraps to motorways—must first be designed. This book was designed to tell you something about designing and help you tackle your own design problems. A television programme is designed to inform or entertain you. Some design problems are simple; some are complicated. Some can be tackled by one person; others require team-work. Behind every man-made article there is a story—the story of a design process. . . .

Thesis: The Torah is a collection of man-made articles that is behind the story of a design process.

18

situation

"HELLO SALLY. IS JANE HERE?"

"NO, SHE SAID SHE WOULDN'T BE ABLE TO MAKE IT TONIGHT"

"SHE HASN'T BEEN HERE FOR A COUPLE OF WEEKS NOW."

"WELL YOU CAN'T BLAME HER. THIS PLACE IS A BIT OF A DUMP."

LATER THAT NIGHT RAY THINKS ABOUT SALLY'S COMMENTS. THE CLUB *WAS* A BIT OF A DUMP. BUT SURELY SOMETHING COULD BE DONE ABOUT IT........

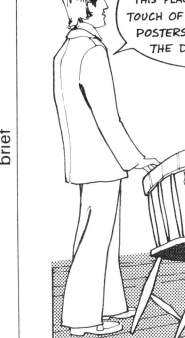

investigation

EVENTUALLY THEY DECIDED TO PAINT THE DOORS AND WINDOWS PURPLE AND THE WALLS WHITE TO MAKE A PLAIN BACKGROUND FOR POSTERS. FOUR OF THE MEMBERS WORKED TOGETHER TO DESIGN AND BUILD A COFFEE BAR IN ONE CORNER OF THE ROOM. A JUMBLE SALE WAS TO BE ARRANGED TO HELP PAY FOR MATERIALS.

"IF WE MADE THIS A BIT LONGER WE COULD PUT THE RECORD PLAYER THERE FOR DANCING"

solution

SALLY SUPERVISED THE CONSTRUCTION OF A SCALE MODEL OF THE ROOM IN CARDBOARD TO SHOW HOW IT WOULD LOOK WHEN FINISHED.....

"HERE ARE THE DRAWINGS AND LIST OF MATERIALS. NOW YOU CAN ORDER THE WOOD AND THE PAINT."

The Sea of Silence

The Budo Dojo

Mu Shy Kyo

THE TAO

situation

brief

investigation

realization

solution

testing

The Bugeisha Master (KODO)

THE PATH - THE WAY

These are aspects of a design process. Now let's look more closely at each of the six stages. . . .

testing

situation

realization

Design

brief

Solution

investigation

23

masakatsu Agatsu

Situation

This is where you find your need to design.

There are many 'situations':

The home

—activities undertaken in the home and in the garden:

equipment and furniture for use in the kitchen, bedroom, garden, etc. interior design.

Other people

—the way they live, work and play:

problems based on the needs of the young, sick, handicapped, aged, etc.

Leisure

—things you do in your spare time:

designing equipment for sports, keeping pets, etc.

The environment

—your surroundings—roads, buildings, parks, the countryside, industry, etc.

work arising from the need for road safety, restoration, problems of unsightly areas, pollution and litter.

A situation could arise from an article in a newspaper . . .

The Future of Bank Hall

The local council met yesterday to discuss the future of Bank Hall. Its present occupiers, the Surveyor's Department, are shortly to move into new offices in the Civic Centre.

The final decision was that because of its historical significance the ten-roomed Georgian house would be retained by the Council and used as a base for handicapped workers.

Mr George Davenport of the Social Services Department, who organizes light working sessions for handicapped people, said that he was delighted with the decision in view of the urgent need for suitable accommodation for his group of handicapped workers. The group has already outgrown the prefabricated buildings in Brooke Place where during the past two years a wide range of products has been made for use in various establishments in town.

Mr Davenport said that in addition to the extra space that this move would provide, his group had a growing need for equipment such as special chairs and work benches.

The chairman of the local planning committee, Mr Oscar Oswald, told our reporter that the proposals considered included using the building as an old people's home, temporary accommodation for immigrants, or a youth club. He said that the Council had also considered selling the site for private factory, office or living accommodation.

It is clear that there would be quite a range of needs arising from the new use of Bank Hall; the article mentions special chairs and workbenches. This is the kind of design problem that could be tackled in a school workshop.

Brief

A brief is a statement of the problem you want to tackle.

A brief may be a short, general statement:

'Produce a toy for children.'

It may be more detailed:

'Produce a toy suitable for children aged between two and four years.'

It may be even more detailed:

'Produce a toy suitable for children aged between two and four years that will encourage them to count and recognize numbers. The toy must be suitable for use in a car on long journeys.'

Of course, if you are drawing up your own **brief** you may start with a short, general statement and then add more detail as you find out more about the problem. In fact this is usually the case when you are designing: as the problem becomes clearer you are better able to see what must be considered.

Eventually you will need to be fairly clear about all the important factors that will affect your answer to the design problem. You will need to make a *complete* description of the problem. This complete description is called a **specification.**

Sometimes your teacher or someone for whom you are making something will give you a specification to which you can work. At other times you will have to produce your own. This is not always easy. It may involve a great deal of enquiry work as indicated in the section dealing with **investigation.**

Generally you will find that your brief will arise out of one of two needs:

— the need to provide something that was not there before;

— the need to improve something that already exists.

What will be the needs of handicapped people working at Bank Hall? You would not be able to draw up a design brief from the information given in the newspaper article. You would have to take some action.

■ Where would you go to get enough information to enable you to draw up a design brief?

■ Who would you talk to?

■ What kind of things would you look for?

These questions do not just apply to Bank Hall. You will need to consider them when producing *any* design brief.

You may find it useful to refer to the questions in this and other sections of the book when *you* are tackling a design problem. Remember that they are not 'test' questions that you have to answer one by one, they are provided simply to remind you of some of the things you may need to consider at some stage during your design process.

Let us look at some of the problem areas in the example given. You would probably discover that many of the handicapped workers are confined to wheelchairs.

— How does a person in a wheelchair get through a door?

— How does a person in a wheelchair work at a bench?

— How does a person in a wheelchair pick things up from the floor?

— How does a person in a wheelchair get up and down steps?

These are just a few of the problems that might exist. Here is a design brief developed from one of these problems:

'Provide a work-bench for a person confined to a wheelchair.'

Investigation

Investigation means finding out more about a design problem, making suggestions for solving each part of the problem and deciding what has to be done and how to do it.

You may already have done some simple investigational work when looking at a situation in order to find a design problem and draw up a design brief. But you will need to know much more about the problem before you can produce a specification or start to think about solutions.

One of the first steps in an investigation will be to ask yourself . . .

■ Who will use the article?

In the example you have been looking at you know that the work-bench will be used by a person in a wheelchair. This person, then, will be one source of the additional information you will need. You need to think of him first as a human being and find out *what he needs* and *why he needs it*.

As you carry on with your investigation you will probably find that your design problem is really made up of several problems. For example, the size of the work-bench, the kinds of jigs, tool-racks, and so on, that may need to be fitted will depend upon what operations are to be carried out there. You must ask yourself . . .

■ How, where and when will the article be used?

If you need to obtain information from several people you may find it helpful to prepare a list of standard questions.

■ How can I record information that will help me understand and solve the problem?

If all this information is to be of any use to you you will have to remember it, but you may find it helpful to record it in some way—by writing, sketching, photographing, filming, tape recording, or any other appropriate method.

By getting to know the problem in this way you will find yourself beginning to think of possible answers. There may be two or three ways in which you could solve the problem. Or there may be dozens.

One way in which designers, craftsmen and engineers begin to sort out their ideas is by sketching them. Each idea or piece of information may be sketched, fairly roughly, several times to show different views or details of construction. Some of the sketches may show only a small part of the item—a joint, perhaps, or part of a mechanism.

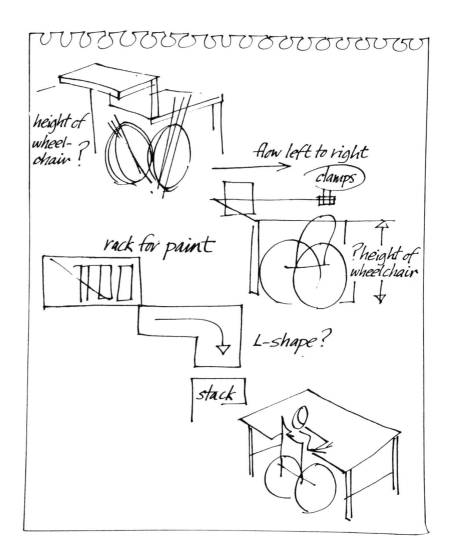

There need be nothing final about these ideas; they are sketched because sketching is a quick and easy method of sorting out ideas.

In the examples illustrated you will see that written notes have been added to some of the sketches. These are to remind the designer of something which might not otherwise be clear from the drawing.

You may not find sketching easy at first. Like all things, it needs practice. You may find—as many people do—that it is simpler to make models of your ideas, using paper, cardboard, wire, expanded polystyrene, or any other easily-worked material. One advantage of a model is that it is easy to see what it looks like from different points of view—you simply turn it around!

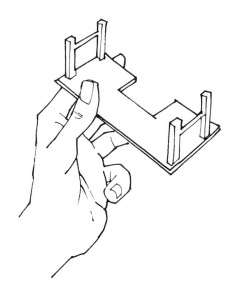

Whichever method you use to explore your ideas it is *very important* that you look for more than one answer to a problem. If you can develop, say, four, five, or even more possibilities then you can examine them and choose which one you think solves the problem best. Or you might combine some parts of one idea with parts of another. If you have only one answer to the problem you cannot do either of these things—because you have nothing to compare it with.

Here are some more general questions you may need to ask yourself during your investigations:

- Can I work through the problem alone, or is a design team needed?

- Do I need to discuss the problem with other people?

- Where can I get more information?

- Shall I need to visit places outside the school?

- Will the article have to be stored? If so, where?

- Will the article have to be moved around?

At some point during your investigation you will find that you are able to make a much more detailed statement of the design problem than that given in the brief. This statement, or specification, is very useful because it helps you to see just what detailed investigation work remains to be done. In addition, it is important to have a clear picture of the problem in mind before you start to think about solutions.

The specification of the Bank Hall work-bench problem might read as follows:

> **'Provide a work-bench for a person confined to a wheelchair. The bench will be used mainly by one person (Mr K. Jenkins) but provision should be made for it to be used by others if necessary. Mr Jenkins makes seed boxes for a local nursery. This involves the following operations:**
> **1 Measuring and sawing off lengths of wood for box sides;**
> **2 Measuring and sawing off rectangle of wood for bottom of box;**
> **3 Holding sides and base in position for nailing;**
> **4 Placing finished seed box on stack for removal.**
> **Further information may be obtained from Mr Jenkins and Mr R. Greene, the foreman.'**

It is important to bear in mind some of the factors that will affect the kind of solution you are looking for. These include:

- Function
- Materials
- Construction
- Appearance
- Cost
- Time

These factors are dealt with in turn in the following pages. You may not need to consider them all in detail, but some of the points raised will almost certainly be relevant to *your* design problem.

Although we have, for convenience, examined these factors separately, there may in fact be a lot of overlap between them. When you are dealing with **function,** for example, you will probably find that you are also thinking about **construction** or **materials.**

When you have thought about these factors you will probably find that your investigation is complete. You are likely to have several ideas in the form of sketches or models.

Function

'Function' means the job something has to do. Any article you are designing may have several jobs to do. This means that you may have to look at several different aspects of function.

It is not possible to deal with all the things you may need to take into account, so we will look at four of the main ones.

Size

An article will not do its job properly if it is the wrong size. Finding out what its dimensions should be is therefore a first step in this area of investigation.

In many design problems there are two aspects of the question of size. This is true of our example of a work-bench for a person confined to a wheelchair. Its size will depend upon what tools and equipment it must hold, and also upon the size of the person using it—how far he or she can reach, what height the bench needs to be for easy working, and so on.

Factors related to the size of the person using an article are part of what are called **ergonomic** factors; these are dealt with on page 38.

> ### SIZE
>
> Work-bench to be used for making seed boxes, enough room required for:
>
> sawing planks to length
> holding wood for hammering
> space for tools and equipment
> space for finished boxes
>
> | size of plank |
>
> ◁——— approx 1.5m ———▷

Sometimes the *inside* dimensions of an article may be important. If the work-bench is to contain drawers or other storage space you will need to find out what items are to be stored and how much space will be required to contain them.

You will need to ask yourself:

■ How can I find out the dimensions of the article I am designing?

Strength

The things we design must be strong enough to do the job they are intended to do. When choosing a material or a method of construction you sometimes have to carry out tests to make sure that it will stand up to the stresses and strains of the real situation.

The work-bench for Bank Hall must be strong enough to support the necessary tools and materials and to stand up to the strain of the hammering and sawing that will be carried out on it.

■ Does the article need to have any particular strengths (or weaknesses)? If so, what are they?

Adaptability

Some products may have to do different things at different times. Our work-bench may have to be used by more than one person, or for more than one operation. For example, you may have to allow for the height of the working surface to be adjusted.

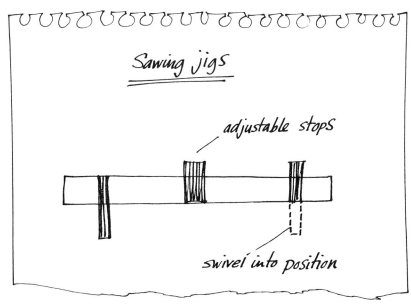

It may be necessary to ask yourself:

■ Will the article need to be used by more than one person or for more than one purpose?

Access

Access may be defined as 'get-at-ability'. In many products, particularly mechanisms, access may be required from time to time to some part that is normally enclosed or otherwise obstructed by some other part of the article. In other words, you may need to 'get at' some part of it in order to service or repair it. Where this is the case access must be made as simple as possible.

Although there are unlikely to be problems of access in the design of a work-bench, there are many other common examples that illustrate this need. The user of this transistor radio can reach and replace the batteries easily because the back of the radio has been designed to slide simply in and out of position.

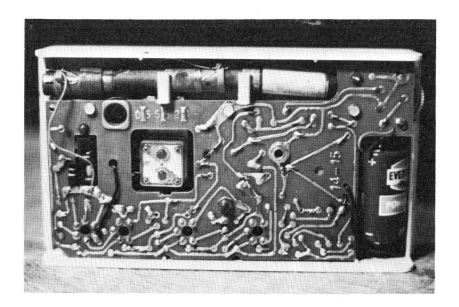

You may have to decide:

■ Will there have to be easy access to enclosed or obstructed parts?

Ergonomics

The things we use are much easier to use if they are made to suit us. Our clothes are more comfortable if they fit. A well-designed telephone is not just one that looks nice and works satisfactorily, it should also be easy to use. For example, the receiver should fit the hand comfortably, the distance between the earpiece and the mouthpiece should suit the distance between our ear and our mouth, and the numbers on the dial should be clear and easy to read.

Factors like these—concerned with the way people use things—are called ergonomic factors.

Ergonomics is very important in the design of the work-bench for Bank Hall. If the height is not convenient it will be uncomfortable, perhaps even dangerous, to use. If the shape is not convenient a person in a wheelchair may not be able to get close enough to it.

The work area and the tools and equipment must be arranged conveniently. Handles and jigs must be made so that they can be used comfortably and safely. Labels and measuring scales must be easy to see and read.

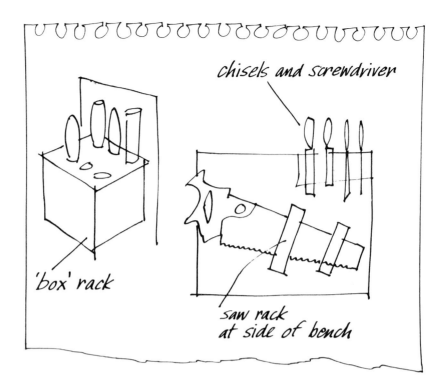

Just as the size and shape of a container is determined by the articles it is to contain, so the sizes and shapes of things to be used by people are found by measuring the people.

When designing an article you are likely to ask:

■ Who will use the article? And in what circumstances?

■ Does it have to be particularly easy to hold, operate or see? If so, what steps do I need to take?

Materials

The materials you choose must be appropriate for the job they have to do.

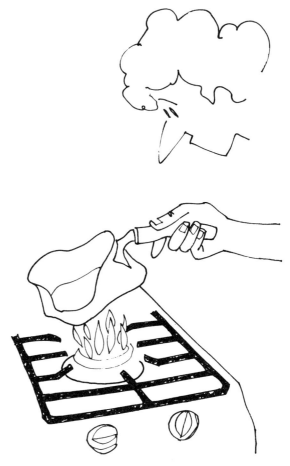

A material must perform satisfactorily.... A substance that melts easily, for example, would be of little use for making saucepans!

An appropriate material is one that is strong enough for the job it has to do, reasonably easy to work, not too expensive, able to perform satisfactorily for as long as necessary, and so on. But first you must find out . . .

- What materials are available?

- What properties do the materials need to have?

- Do I need to make any simple tests on materials to check strength or other properties?

You must also use a material in a way that is appropriate to its structure and its particular characteristics. You cannot, for example, treat woods as if they were metals, or glass as if it were cardboard.

You will need to decide:

- Have I the necessary skills to work the materials available?

Sometimes you may need to use a hard material, or a soft one; a flexible one, or a rigid one; a heavy one, or a light one. Ease of working, too, may be important. You may need to carry out tests to check the suitability of a material.

You will also have to work out how much material you need. It may be helpful to prepare a chart so that these details can be recorded conveniently and accurately.

Part	Material	Size	No. required
legs	pine	75 mm square × 1 m	6
	or slotted angle	62 × 41 × 2 mm × 1 m	6

POSSIBLE MATERIALS

top: wood or plastic?

legs: wood, angle iron, slotted angle metal tube

racks: wood, plastic? (leather strap for saw?)

Construction

The construction you use for a job—that is, the way you put the parts together—must be appropriate.

No firm ideas about construction can be developed until a material has been selected. Different materials have different properties and characteristics and these will determine how you can join them together.

When you come to design the construction of an article you should have one main aim—to make it as effective as possible without complication or waste.

There are several advantages in doing this:

— you may save material, and money;

— you may need fewer connections, and therefore save time;

— you may need less work altogether, and therefore save effort.

Here is an example. These wooden stools are each made of nine pieces of material and have twelve connections.

But this metal stool, which does a similar job, is made of only eight pieces of material and four connections. The work required to make the stool is less so time, money and materials have all been saved.

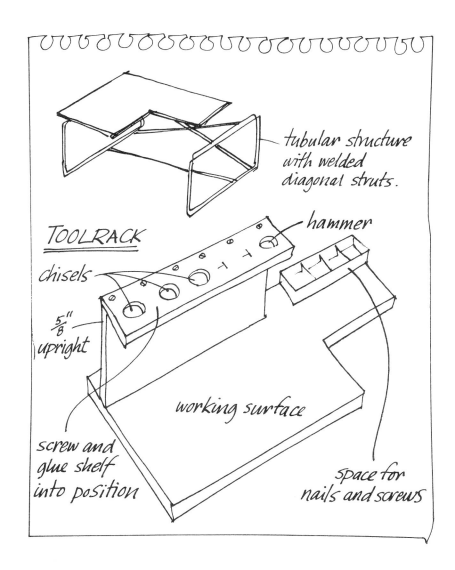

Here are some of the things you may need to consider:

- What methods of construction do I need to explore?
- Shall I need to test construction methods to check strength or any other requirement?
- Is it possible to use fewer joints and fewer parts in order to keep the article simple?
- Do I want to make constructional details visible, or should they be hidden?

Appearance

Sometimes an article has a pleasing appearance just because it works well and uses a simple construction with appropriate materials. Craftsmen sometimes say an article 'looks right'. At other times you have to make deliberate choices about the shape and form of parts, the combination of colours and textures, and so on, for the sake of the overall appearance.

The way a thing **looks** arouses different feelings in different people. What may be attractive to some may be unattractive to others. So you can see there are no hard and fast rules about this.

Whatever you may think about an object, you should always try to find out **why** you like or dislike it.

Many people find the sleek form of the Concorde attractive. But in fact the desire for a pleasing appearance played little part in its design. This is an example of good looks resulting from the demands of function: the sleek form of the Concorde owes more to aerodynamics than to art.

In most design problems a product's appearance will result from considerations of function *and* use of materials (as well as the designer's own likes and dislikes). These simple forms work well, they are comfortable to hold and use, and the designer's appreciation of the characteristics of stainless steel have led to products that are economic to make and (most people would agree) pleasant to look at.

Although there are no hard and fast rules about appearance there is one word worth bearing in mind. That word is *appropriateness*. Whatever you do when cutting shapes, combining colours, or making surfaces rough or smooth you should try to make it appropriate to the kind of article, its function, its surroundings and the materials you are using.

It may take some time before you can decide what appearance an article should have. As in other areas of your work you may need to make models or sketches, or conduct experiments to see, for example, which combinations of materials or shapes work well.

You may find that some of the decisions you have already taken about function, materials or construction limit what you can do. Or it may be that what you decide about appearance may lead you to think again about a decision you took earlier.

In other words, a certain amount of 'juggling' may be necessary—balancing a neat appearance with the need for a strong construction, for example.

Don't forget that different people have different ideas about appearance. If, as in the work-bench example, you are making something for someone else it may be important to find out if they have particular preferences or dislikes. (And if so, why.)

You may need to ask:

■ Will I need to consult anyone about appearance?

■ Will the surroundings affect the appearance of the article?

■ If there are any large surfaces do they need 'breaking up' (visually) to make them more interesting to look at?

Cost

Cost is a very important factor in any kind of design work. An idea may be acceptable in every other way, but if it is too expensive to make, or for someone to buy, then the designer has failed in his task.

It is wise to make sure that the cost of materials will be acceptable before making the final choice of solution. You may find it helpful to draw up a chart so that the cost of each part can be seen and a total cost worked out.

Part	Material	Size	No. required	Cost
legs	pine	75 mm square × 1 m	6	£0.60
	or slotted angle	62 × 41 × 2 mm × 1 m	6	Standard 30-metre pack: £16.00

You may have to consider:

■ Who is paying for the materials?

■ When will the materials have to be paid for?

■ Has any limit been placed on the cost of the end-product?

■ How much would it cost to make the article?

In certain circumstances there may be a commercially-available product to suit a need or problem. . . .

■ Would it be possible to buy a suitable product?

Time

Time, like cost, is an all-important factor in many design problems. An article that takes too long to design and make may be as of little use as one which is too expensive.

The amount of time spent on the various stages of design and construction must be planned carefully. Sometimes you may be given a time plan, at other times you will have to draw up your own.

You may need to decide:

■ How much time is available?

■ How will I allocate my time?

<u>TIME</u>
Total for 1 term (28 hours)
① Plan procedure ⎱ 1 lesson
② Obtain materials ⎰
③ Make supports and struts   approx $3\frac{1}{2}$ hrs
④ Make top   " $1\frac{1}{2}$ hrs
⑤ Make jigs and fittings   " $7\frac{1}{2}$ hrs
⑥ Assemble   "   5 hrs
⑦ Finishing   "   3 hrs
⑧ Delivery ⎱ 4 hrs
⑨ Testing ⎰
   Allow for hold-ups $1\frac{1}{2}$ hrs

Solution

At this stage the idea is selected which best suits the needs of the design problem.

There comes a time when it is necessary to decide which of the lines followed during an investigation offers the best chance of leading to a satisfactory end-product.

- Can any suggestions be ruled out for any reason?
- Which of the remaining ideas seem most suitable or most promising?

Close examination may reveal some good points in several ideas, so you may wish to combine different ideas to form a new solution. If so, you are probably thinking quite hard about those ideas. You will be checking that all the requirements are covered.

Don't forget that it should be possible to make, or 'realize', the solution you choose using the equipment and materials available.

- Are parts of some ideas worth selecting?

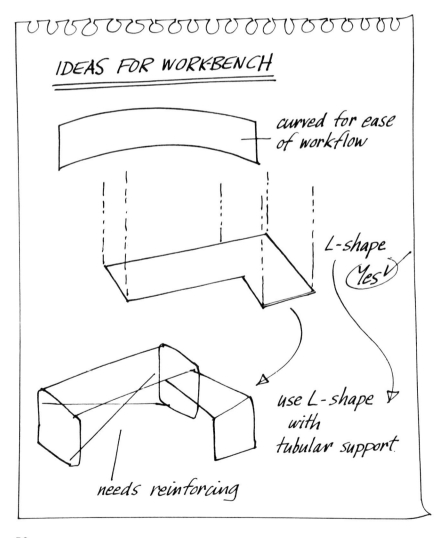

Once you have made your choice you may find it helpful to build a full-size prototype or scale model so that you are able to see certain details that may not have been clear in earlier sketches or models.

Whether or not you decide to make a prototype, it is important to make sure that you have sufficient accurate information to be able to make the article. It can be frustrating to spend weeks making a table and then find it won't go through the door of the room it was designed for!

Another way to smooth production is to prepare a *working drawing* of your product. This shows details of the size of parts, their precise positions, the way in which they are joined together and the materials from which they are made. You may find it helpful to prepare a list of all parts and their sizes to accompany this master drawing.

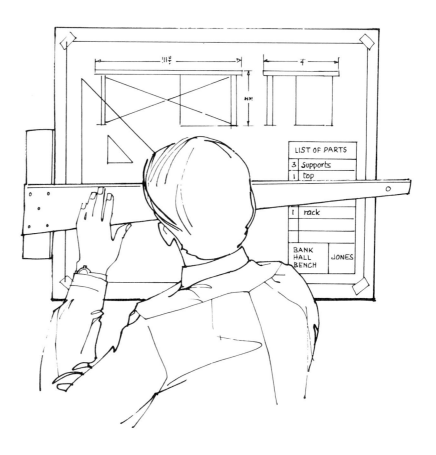

If the article is drawn full size it may be possible to use the drawing as a pattern for checking sizes and shapes—by putting the actual pieces of material on the drawing to see if they match.

- What is the best way of presenting all the information needed to make the article?

- Will it be necessary to make a model or full-size prototype as an aid to the manufacturing stage?

Realization

'Realizing' a design solution means making the article that has been designed.

It may often take a considerable amount of time to make an article; careful planning will help keep this to a minimum. It may also prevent delays due to some special tool or material not being ordered well before the day it is needed.

Before starting work you should be sure that you understand all the requirements of the job you are about to tackle and have some idea of how long it will take you to finish it. Unless you do this you may find that there isn't enough time to get the work finished, and you may find yourself rushing and spoiling what you have already done.

- Where will the materials come from?
- Will I need any special materials, tools or equipment?
- Will it be necessary to set up any special work areas for certain operations?
- In what order will the various parts be made?
- What kinds of skills and knowledge do I need to make the article?
- Do I have enough skill and knowledge to make the article?
- What new things do I need to learn?

If you have a definite deadline, a fairly strict time schedule may have to be drawn up. Don't forget to make regular checks to see that you are on target!

- Do I need to work to a time schedule?

Remember that the most common operations may involve:

— holding the material firmly while you work on it;

— cutting or forming the material;

— joining the material together;

— finishing the material.

Where difficult shapes need to be made you should allow time to prepare templates or jigs. These may take up time at the beginning but will speed things up later—especially where the same operation has to be done a number of times.

- What jigs or templates will be required?

As at other stages of a design process it may be necessary to work with other people in a production team. Where this is the case it is important that each person knows exactly what has to be done at each stage.

As practical work progresses you may think of better ideas for certain parts of the job. Before making any changes or modifications check that they can be carried out without too much trouble. If you are working as a member of a team don't forget to tell other people about the change and make all necessary alterations to the working drawing or prototype.

Testing

Testing is carried out to see how well an article performs. In other words, to see whether it meets the need or solves the problem outlined in the design brief or specification.

In order to find out how well your product does the job it was intended to do, you must first be clear about what that job is.

■ What function is the article meant to perform? (Information collected during your investigation should enable you to answer this question.)

It may be necessary for you to decide the *degree* of success of your product. It may perform its function:

— very well;

— fairly well;

— badly

You will also need to find out *why* your product performs as it does. In deciding how successful your design work has been you may find it helpful to carry out a range of tests. Some of these may be simple, others may be more difficult to undertake. Remember that:

— an article may need to be put under test conditions for a period of time;

— a series of visits may have to be made to observe the article being used in its proper setting;

— you will probably need to find out what other people think of the article (including, of course, the user or users);

— in some cases it may be possible to set up test conditions that represent the real conditions under which an article will be used in order to test it conveniently and accurately.

■ What tests will be needed to check the performance of your product?

If you have to carry out a number of tests, or if a test is long or complicated, you may need to record the results in some form. Perhaps you will find it helpful to draw up a questionnaire or list of points covering each part of the article.

> ### WORK-BENCH TEST
> —Points to check
>
> ① Opinion of user.
> ② Opinion of foreman.
> ③ Watch operation to see that user is able to work effectively as planned.
> ④ Has bench modified the way the user works?
> ⑤ Does the jig produce a satisfactory job?
> ⑥ Does the jig stand up to continuous use?

■ How will you record and analyse your test results?

■ Can you suggest any ways in which your design could be modified or improved as a result of your tests?

Design in daily life

So far you have been mainly concerned with design problems which involve *making* something. But these are not the only problems in which a design process can be useful to you. The various stages of situation, brief, investigation, and so on, are found in some form or other in many kinds of problems—problems in which a *plan of action* can play an important and helpful part.

Here are two situations in which a plan of action may be helpful:

1 Repairing a car. What operations do you need to carry out? In what order?

2 Buying a toy. What do you need? What is available? What can you afford?

Think about this example:

situation

It's a cold, wet, windy evening. You are waiting for a bus, wishing you were at home in front of a warm fire.

brief

You decide you need a car.

Thinking about the problem a little more you come to the conclusion that what you would like is a white sports car with a folding hood for summer days.

investigation

Should you rush at the next opportunity and buy the first car you see? Or should you look at a range of different cars and compare them?

The answer is obvious. Whether you are buying a car, a washing machine, a carpet or a hi-fi set you must make a thorough investigation. A choice made after a few minutes thought is not likely to be a very good choice. In fact it could be a very expensive one.

If you consider all the facts carefully you have a much better chance of choosing the car which suits you best and is good value for money.

Among the things you will have to think about are: how much you can afford to pay for the car, how much it will cost to run and keep in good repair, how many passengers you may need to carry, and what additional equipment (if any) you will need.

If you had followed this plan of action carefully you would probably be satisfied with your purchases.

In this example no end-product was actually manufactured; the solution was 'realized' when the car was bought.

Sometimes the stages of your design process may be dealt with in a different order. In the above example testing may have been included at the investigation stage—perhaps by arranging trial runs in several cars. In addition, for as long as you owned the car you would be testing it and gaining more experience, so that the next time you bought a car you might be able to make an even better choice.

Essentially, the purpose of a design process is to help you to make decisions—decisions, perhaps, about what to make or buy to satisfy a particular need. In fact the basic process described in this book is sometimes called the problem-solving or decision-making process. It is a plan of action that can be adapted to help you in a variety of situations:

- when you need to MAKE something;

- when you need to BUY something;

- when you need to ORGANIZE something;

- when you need to FORM AN OPINION about something.

It is a process you can use when making decisions with and for others as well as for yourself.

In our lives today we can see that all these decisions are linked. What we decide to do in our own gardens doesn't just affect *us*. It may also raise problems for other people. Will our much-wanted pigeon loft be an 'eyesore' to our neighbours? Will the birds annoy other people? We may even have to take the planning bye-laws into account in this case, and we shall certainly have to consider the needs and opinions of others.

In short, designing is not just something you do by yourself for yourself, it is something that very often affects your fellow men.

Some very difficult designing and decision making—concerned with the need for houses, roads, bridges, and so on—has always been done by specialists such as architects, engineers, surveyors, building society officers, housing managers and building developers.

These experts, and many others like them, are taking decisions that affect us all—they are influencing the way we live because they are changing our environment.

If you care to understand about designing and decision making you are more likely to be able to take part in the decisions that are being made on your behalf—to share in them instead of simply being on the receiving end. If you can talk with and express your views to the specialists you may be able to understand and share in their decisions.